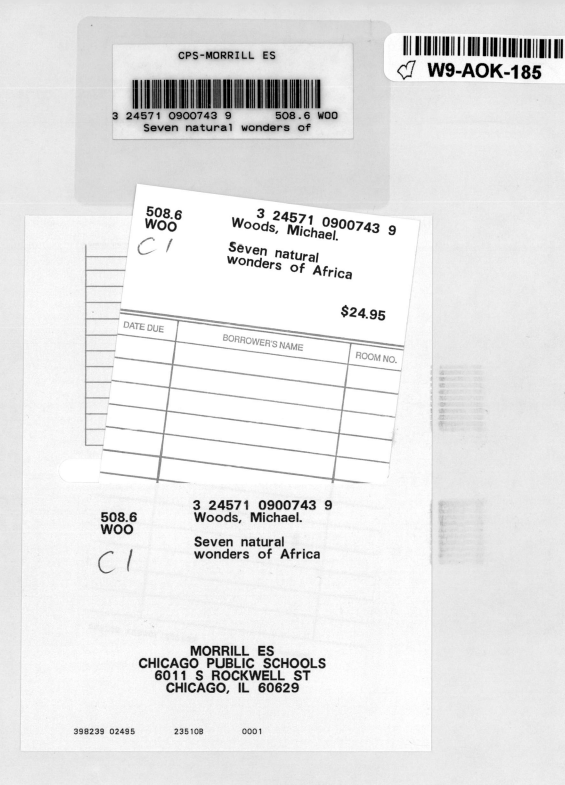

508.6
WOO

3 24571 0900743 9
Woods, Michael.

C I

Seven natural
wonders of Africa

$24.95

DATE DUE	BORROWER'S NAME	ROOM NO.

508.6
WOO

3 24571 0900743 9
Woods, Michael.

C I

Seven natural
wonders of Africa

Seven Natural Wonders of
AFRICA

Michael Woods and Mary B. Woods

TWENTY-FIRST CENTURY BOOKS

Minneapolis

To Robert and Gail Meighan

Twenty-First Century Books
A division of Lerner Publishing Group, Inc.
241 First Avenue North
Minneapolis, MN 55401 U.S.A.

Website address: www.lernerbooks.com

Library of Congress Cataloging-in-Publication Data

Woods, Michael, 1946–
      Seven natural wonders of Africa / by Michael Woods and Mary B. Woods.
          p.   cm. – (Seven wonders)
      Includes bibliographical references and index.
      ISBN 978-0-8225-9071-2 (lib. bdg. : alk. paper)
        1. Natural history—Africa—Juvenile literature. 2. Landforms—Africa—Juvenile literature. 3. Mountains—Africa—Juvenile literature. 4. Bodies of water—Africa—Juvenile literature. 5. Deserts—Africa—Juvenile literature. 6. Curiosities and wonders—Africa—Juvenile literature. 7. Africa—Geography—Juvenile literature. 8. Africa—History, Local—Juvenile literature. I. Woods, Mary B. (Mary Boyle), 1946– II. Title.
      QH194.W66 2009
      508.6–dc22   2008021867

Manufactured in the United States of America
1 2 3 4 5 6 – DP – 14 13 12 11 10 09

Contents

INTRODUCTION

*P*EOPLE LOVE TO MAKE LISTS OF THE BIGGEST AND THE BEST. ALMOST 2,500 YEARS AGO, A GREEK WRITER NAMED HERODOTUS MADE A LIST OF THE MOST AWESOME THINGS EVER BUILT BY PEOPLE. THE LIST INCLUDED BUILDINGS, STATUES, AND OTHER OBJECTS THAT WERE LARGE, WONDROUS, AND IMPRESSIVE. LATER, OTHER WRITERS ADDED NEW ITEMS TO THE LIST. WRITERS EVENTUALLY AGREED ON A FINAL LIST. IT WAS CALLED THE SEVEN WONDERS OF THE ANCIENT WORLD.

The list became so famous that people began imitating it. They made other lists of wonders. They listed Seven Wonders of the Modern World and Seven Wonders of the Middle Ages. People even made lists of undersea wonders.

People also made lists of natural wonders. Natural wonders are extraordinary things created by nature, without help from people. Earth is full of natural wonders, so it has been hard for people to choose the absolute best. Over the years, different people have made different lists of the Seven Wonders of the Natural World.

This book explores seven natural wonders from the continent of Africa. Like Earth as a whole, Africa has far more than seven natural wonders. But even if people can never agree on which ones are the greatest, these seven choices are sure to amaze you.

A WONDERFUL CONTINENT

Africa is the world's second-largest continent after Asia. It covers about 20 percent of Earth's total land area. Africa stretches about 5,000 miles (8,000 kilometers) from north to south. It measures about 4,600 miles (7,400 km) from east to west. It takes about ten hours to fly across Africa in a jetliner. The countries of China, India, and the United States would all fit inside Africa—with plenty of room left over. More than 900 million people live in Africa, more than any other continent except Asia.

Africa has a variety of fascinating natural features. They range from dry deserts in the north to vast rain forests in the center of the continent. Africa also abounds with living wonders. Zebras and wildebeests travel across the grasslands of Tanzania's Serengeti Plain. Mountain gorillas live in the Virunga Mountains in eastern Africa.

WONDERFUL ADVENTURE

This book will take you on a tour of Africa's natural wonders. One stop on the tour will be at the world's longest river—the Nile. In ancient times, the Nile was home to Egyptian kings and pyramids. In modern times, millions of people, plants, and animals still make their homes near the river. Another stop will be at Victoria Falls. This magnificent sheet of falling water is on the Zambezi River between Zambia and Zimbabwe. The tour will also visit the world's biggest hot desert, the Sahara. It is one of the hottest places on Earth—with some of the highest temperatures ever recorded. Another highlight on the tour will be the ancient island country of the Seychelles, with its collection of magical plants and animals. Other fascinating places are waiting in between these visits. Read on to begin your adventure.

The world's biggest hot desert is the Sahara.

1 MOUNTAIN *Gorillas*

A group of mountain gorillas grazes in the Rwandan forest. Few people knew about the gorillas until scientist Dian Fossey brought her research into the public eye in the 1970s.

$\mathcal{I}$N 1967 DIAN FOSSEY, A U.S. BIOLOGIST, SET UP A RESEARCH CENTER IN THE AFRICAN NATION OF RWANDA. SHE HAD COME TO STUDY MOUNTAIN GORILLAS. PREVIOUSLY, SCIENTISTS HAD STUDIED THESE ANIMALS BY WATCHING THEM FOR SHORT PERIODS. FOSSEY STUDIED THE GORILLAS BY LIVING AMONG THEM FOR YEARS AT A TIME. SHE SAT AMONG GORILLAS DAY AFTER DAY AND WATCHED THEIR BEHAVIOR. TO KEEP TRACK OF THE GORILLAS, SHE GAVE THEM NAMES. IN 1970 PHOTOGRAPHS OF A GORILLA NAMED PEANUTS TOUCHING FOSSEY'S HAND MADE HER FAMOUS AROUND THE WORLD.

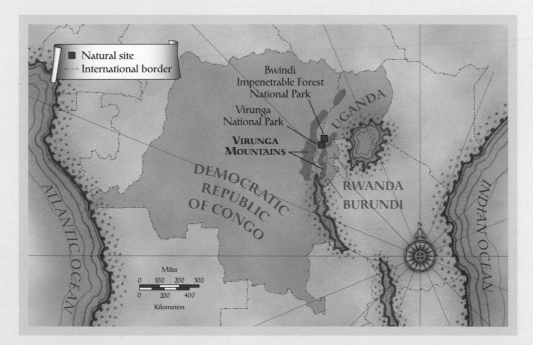

Dian Fossey sits with a group of young mountain gorillas in 1982. She named her gorilla research station Karisoke, combining the names of two nearby volcanoes, Mount Karisimbi and Mount Visoke.

Dian Fossey's research station was in the Virunga Mountains. These mountains lie in Rwanda, Uganda, and the Democratic Republic of Congo (DRC). The mountains are one of only two remaining habitats, or natural homes, for mountain gorillas. The other habitat is the Bwindi Impenetrable Forest in Uganda.

Mountain gorillas are one of three kinds of gorillas. The other two are western lowland gorillas and eastern lowland gorillas. All gorillas are big and hairy. But mountain gorillas have longer, thicker hair than lowland gorillas. Their jaws and teeth are larger. Mountain gorillas have black hair. Lowland gorillas have brownish gray hair.

Mountain gorillas are also far less numerous than lowland gorillas. Scientists think that thousands of lowland gorillas live in the rain forests of central and western Africa. Mountain gorillas number fewer than eight hundred.

BIG AND PEACEFUL

Gorillas belong to an animal group called apes. This group also includes bonobos, chimpanzees, gibbons, and orangutans. Apes are humans' closest relatives in the animal kingdom. Apes are part of a larger animal group called primates. The primate group includes people.

WHAT'S IN A *Name?*

Before Europeans arrived, local people of the Virunga Mountains had various names for gorillas. The name *gorilla* **was the invention of Thomas Staughton Savage, a U.S. naturalist and missionary (religious teacher). Savage traveled to Africa in the 1830s and 1840s. In 1847 he wrote the first description of a gorilla. He picked the name** *gorilla* **from an ancient Greek story. The story tells of the Gorillai, a tribe of hairy women.**

Gorillas are the largest primates. Male gorillas can weigh up to 350 pounds (159 kilograms). Standing on their hind legs, they can measure 6 feet (2 meters) tall. Females weigh about 215 pounds (98 kg) and stand about 5 feet (1.5 m) in height. An adult gorilla may eat 40 pounds (18 kg) of bamboo shoots, wild celery, fruit, and other plants each day.

Gorillas live in groups of up to thirty members. Each group has males, females, and youngsters. The group leader is a large adult male. When young gorillas are old enough to reproduce, they usually leave the group to find mates.

Right: *A mountain gorilla grazes in the jungle.* Below: *A male gorilla watches over two female gorillas* (right) *and two young gorillas* (left). *Adult male gorillas tell the group when to graze, rest, and move on.*

Gorillas spend the day peacefully munching on food and resting. Sometimes, however, the group leader needs to take charge. To keep order or to scare off enemies, the leader will howl, scream, charge, throw sticks, or beat his chest.

GORILLA MOUNTAINS

The Virunga Mountains once provided an ideal home for mountain gorillas. The mountains have fertile soil and lots of plants for gorillas to eat. In earlier centuries, few people bothered the gorillas in the Virunga Mountains. Local Africans told frightening stories about the mountains. They said that giant alligators and human-eating plants lived there. People were afraid to enter the mountains. Leopards were the only animals that preyed on the mountain gorillas.

Eventually, though, people made their way into the mountains. In the 1800s, hunters from Europe and the United States began traveling to Africa. They shot gorillas and other large animals for sport. Hunters often displayed the skins, heads, and horns of animals they had killed. Some hunters even turned gorilla hands and feet into ashtrays. Sometimes Africans from the surrounding area also killed mountain gorillas for food.

In the early 1920s, hunters killed fifty mountain gorillas in the Virunga Mountains. When news of the slaughter reached Europe, people were concerned. They worried that mountain gorillas might become extinct, or die out altogether. To protect the animals, government leaders created two national parks.

GREAT *Ape*

Fans of King Kong movies will notice that the giant gorilla has changed over the years. In the first *King Kong*, made in 1933, Kong ate people, beat his chest with clenched fists, stood upright, and walked on two feet like a human. In the most recent *King Kong*, made in 2005, Kong ate plants not people. He walked on all fours, using his front legs like an extra pair of feet. Kong beat his chest with cupped hands. Kong was still a gigantic, fantastical creature. But he acted more like a real gorilla *(below)*.

Dian Fossey
speaks with her
favorite gorilla,
Digit. Fossey
used a combina-
tion of noises
and hand signals
to communicate
with the gorillas.

The first was in the Virunga Mountains. The second was in the Bwindi Impenetrable Forest.

The national parks were supposed to be off-limits to hunters. But people continued to hunt gorillas illegally. By the 1950s, only about three hundred mountain gorillas were left in the Virunga Mountains. Another three hundred lived in the Bwindi Impenetrable Forest.

MYSTERIOUS Death

In 1985 someone murdered Dian Fossey in her cabin in the Virunga Mountains. Some people suspect that hunters killed her, but no one is sure. Fossey was buried next to Digit, her favorite gorilla, in a cemetery used for her dead gorilla friends. The words "No one loved gorillas more" are carved on her gravestone.

EXTRA PROTECTION

In the late 1900s, scientists such as Dian Fossey tried to protect mountain gorillas. After hunters killed one of her favorite gorillas, Digit, Fossey organized patrols of armed guards to keep hunters away. Fossey also used her red hair to frighten away local hunters. At the time, most African people had never seen a redhead. Some hunters thought that Fossey was a witch who could jinx them with evil spells. Fossey encouraged that belief to frighten hunters.

Fossey's work made more people realize that mountain gorillas needed protection. In 1979 the United Nations Educational, Scientific, and Cultural

Organization (UNESCO) named Virunga National Park a World Heritage Site. World Heritage Sites are places of great importance to all humanity. UNESCO tries to protect and preserve these sites for future generations.

But mountain gorillas were still not safe from human beings. In the late 1900s, wars raged in places near the Virunga Mountains. To escape the fighting, people fled to forests in the mountains. They cut down trees to use as cooking fuel. In the 1990s, during a war in Rwanda, about forty thousand people cut firewood in Virunga National Park. They cut almost 2 million pounds (910,000 kg) of wood each day.

Refugees from war in Rwanda carry wood out of the Virunga National Park. In the 1990s, thousands of displaced people moved into huge tent cities near the edge of the forest. Many walked for hours to gather wood for cooking and to build shelters.

With the trees gone, the mountain gorillas had fewer places to live. In addition, people continued to hunt gorillas. In 2007 hunters killed at least ten gorillas in the Virunga Mountains

Despite these problems, mountain gorillas have managed to survive. In 2007 scientists reported that the number of mountain gorillas was increasing by about 1 percent every year. In 2008 scientists counted about 720 mountain gorillas in the Virunga Mountains and the Bwindi Impenetrable Forest.

"If humankind wishes to share this planet with the apes in centuries to come we can never ignore their existence. . . . We must cherish and protect the gorillas forevermore."
—biologist George Beals Schaller, 1963

A group of mountain gorillas grazes at the edge of a field in Virunga National Park.

2 THE Nile River

In this image, the Nile River cuts through the wilderness of Uganda. The southern section of the river flows through forests and farming regions. The northern part of the river provides the only water in vast desert areas.

Some natural wonders are famous for being big or beautiful or for providing a home for rare animals and plants. The Nile River in Africa is famous for being long. Geographers think that the Nile is the world's longest river. It flows for nearly 4,200 miles (6,700

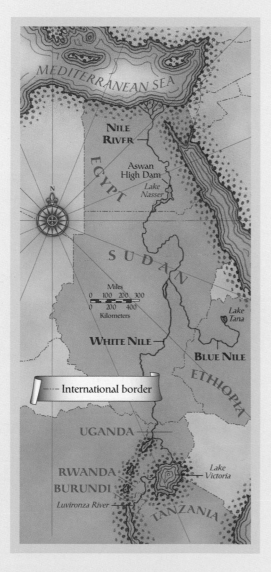

km) through Egypt and other African countries. This river is long enough to reach from New York City to Los Angeles and more than two-thirds of the way back.

The Nile flows through deserts, dense jungles, and steep canyons. The Nile has spectacular waterfalls. It has rapids where water churns, roars, and foams over rocks. Hippos, crocodiles, fish, baboons, elephants, rhinos, falcons, cranes, herons, and other animals live in the Nile or along its banks.

A yellow-billed stork searches for fish in the Nile as a small crocodile swims nearby. The river supports thousands of species of plants and animals.

The modern name *Nile* comes from the Greek word *neilos*, which means "valley." The Nile does flow through an enormous valley. The river has carved out the valley over millions of years. In some spots, the Nile valley is a flat area almost 30 miles (48 km) wide. In some places, rocky walls tower above each side of the valley. The walls are up to 800 feet (244 m) high.

RIVER OF LIFE

The Nile did something that few other natural wonders can match. This river changed world history. The Nile gave us one of the world's greatest civilizations—ancient Egypt. Without the Nile, there would have been no pharaohs (Egyptian kings), no pyramids (tombs for pharaohs), and no Egyptian mummies.

People began to settle in villages along the Nile around 5000 B.C. Egypt receives very little rainfall, so the Nile provided the only reliable source of water for these villages. Water from the Nile allowed people to raise farm animals and to grow wheat, figs, onions, and other crops. People also used the river's water for drinking, cooking, and washing.

SUMMER *Jobs*

Most ancient Egyptians were farmers. When the Nile flooded in summer, farmers could not work in their fields. Instead, some worked for the pharaoh (king). They helped build the pharaoh's pyramids and other structures. Other farmers joined the pharaoh's army and fought to conquer surrounding territories.

HAPY MADE THEM HAPPY

Farming requires fertile soil. In ancient Egypt, the Nile provided it in great abundance. Every year between June and August, the Nile overflowed its banks, flooding the surrounding farmland. When the floods stopped in September or October, the Nile shrank back within its banks. But it left a coating of rich soil on the land. The soil was perfect for growing crops.

At floodtime in Egypt, the Nile looked like a thick black soup. It was loaded with rich soil that had washed into the river as it flowed through other parts of Africa. Because of the color, ancient Egyptians called the Nile *Ar*, which meant "black" in their language.

The yearly flooding of the Nile was a mystery to the ancient Egyptians. The floods happened in the middle of burning hot summers, when temperatures soared above 110°F (43°C) and not a drop of rain fell. The Egyptians thought that their gods provided the water. They worshipped a flood god named Hapy.

The Egyptians didn't know that the yearly floods actually started far upriver. Rainy weather in places south of Egypt caused the Nile to swell with water. When the river reached Egypt, it overflowed its banks.

"Hail to thee, O Nile! Who manifests [shows] thyself over this land, and comes to give life to Egypt!"
—from "Hymn to the Nile," an ancient Egyptian song, ca. 2100 B.C.

LONG, LONG RIVER

Although the Nile makes many people think of Egypt, less than one-fourth of this mighty river—960 miles (1,545 km)—flows through Egypt. Most of the Nile flows through other African countries. The Nile begins in Burundi in east central Africa. It flows north through Uganda and Sudan before finally reaching Egypt.

In southern Sudan, the Nile is called the White Nile. At Khartoum, the capital of Sudan, the White Nile joins with a river called the Blue Nile. Together they form one mighty river that flows northward into Egypt. In northern Egypt, the Nile divides into many smaller rivers right before it flows into the Mediterranean Sea.

The White Nile and the Blue Nile divide the city of Khartoum, Sudan, into three parts. The place where the rivers meet is called al-Mogran, which means "the horn" in Arabic. At that point, the milky waters of the White Nile (left) combine with the clearer Blue Nile (right) around a horn-shaped piece of land.

WATER *Colors*

The Blue Nile is named for its water, which looks blue black during the flood season. The White Nile is also named for the color of its water. The river carries particles of whitish gray clay, which give the water a milky gray color.

EVER *Wonder?*

Why the Nile River flows from south to north? The Nile flows in that direction because it is downhill. The Nile's water starts flowing from mountains and other high ground in the middle of Africa. The land slopes downhill into southern Egypt. The land slopes down farther into northern Egypt and the Mediterranean Sea.

The ancient Egyptians divided their country into Upper Egypt and Lower Egypt. Upper Egypt was the southern half of the country. Lower Egypt was the north. These labels confuse some people—because on maps, north is higher than south. But the division makes perfect sense. Upper Egypt had a higher altitude (height above sea level) than Lower Egypt.

SEARCH FOR THE SOURCE

In modern times, geographers have thoroughly mapped the Nile. But for thousands of years, the Nile was one of the world's greatest geographical mysteries. Rulers of ancient Egypt, Rome, and Greece sent armies marching up the Nile to find its starting point.

In A.D. 150, the Alexandrian astronomer Ptolemy heard stories from travelers who had visited the Nile. He thought that the Nile's source was in the Mountains of the Moon. This group of mountains sits near the border of present-day Democratic Republic of Congo and Uganda. Ptolemy's idea was only a guess, however, and it was incorrect.

In 1618 a Spanish priest named Pedro Páez discovered that a spring in Ethiopia was the source of the Blue Nile. That spring flows into Ethiopia's Lake Tana. The Blue Nile flows out of Lake Tana.

The source of the Nile itself remained a mystery. Explorers had a hard time solving that mystery. They traveled south on the Nile in riverboats. But six big rapids blocked their way. At the rapids, rocks, roaring waves, and strong currents overturned their boats.

"It was said of Alexander the Great [a Greek general who conquered Egypt] that the first question he asked . . . was where the Nile had its [source], and we know he sent discoverers throughout Ethiopia without being able to [find] this source."

—*Portuguese writer Baltazar Tellez, 1710*

The Blue Nile flows out of Lake Tana and crashes over Blue Nile Falls in Ethiopia. In the Ethiopian language of Amharic, the falls are known as Tis Issat, which means "water and smoke."

Left: *John Speke stands with his surveying equipment in front of Lake Victoria in 1858.*
Right: *The search for the source of the Nile led explorers to this waterfall on the shores of Lake Victoria.*

To get around the rapids, explorers sometimes walked along the Nile's banks. They had to walk through swamps and jungles. These were dangerous places. Mosquitoes and other blood-sucking insects lived in the swamps. Poisonous snakes and other dangerous animals lived in the jungles. Sometimes, local people attacked the explorers. Some explorers who tried to follow the river south disappeared and were never heard from again.

John Speke was a British explorer. In 1858 he was the first European to reach Lake Victoria in east central Africa. Speke thought that Lake Victoria was the source of the Nile. Several rivers flow into Lake Victoria. Modern geographers have determined that one of these rivers, the Luvironza in Burundi, is the ultimate source of the Nile.

A MODERN WONDER

The Nile remains the river of life for modern Egypt. The river crosses about 5 percent of Egypt's land. However, 95 percent of Egypt's people live near the river. Altogether, about 105 million people live along the Nile. Most of these people live in Egypt.

Flooding no longer occurs along the Nile because of the Aswan High Dam. Built in the 1960s, the dam prevents floods by blocking the Nile. Instead of flowing freely downstream, the water collects in a huge lake behind the dam. The lake, Lake Nasser, stretches 310 miles (500 km) south into Sudan. The dam releases water from Lake Nasser slowly, so that none spills over the riverbanks and causes floods. Water flowing through the dam turns electric generators, creating most of Egypt's electricity. Egyptians also use water from the lake at their homes and farms.

WHICH IS *Longer?*

For many years, scientists thought that the Amazon River in South America was 4,000 miles (6,436 km) long, about 200 miles (322 km) shorter than the Nile. But in 2007, a team of scientists claimed to have found a more distant source for the Amazon. They say the Amazon is really 4,250 miles (6,838 km) long. If these scientists are correct, the Amazon is longer than the Nile and is the longest river in the world.

The Aswan High Dam (right) is the second dam built near the Sudanese city of Aswan. In 1902 British engineers completed the first dam, known as the Aswan Low Dam.

The creation of Lake Nasser threatened many archaeological sites along the Nile. The lake covers the ruins on Philae Island for most of the year. These ruins include Trajan's Kiosk (above), a memorial to the Roman emperor Trajan, who died in A.D. 117. (The Romans ruled parts of northern Africa between the third century B.C. and the fifth century A.D.)

South of the Nile, many African nations have experienced droughts—periods of little or no rainfall. These long dry periods have reduced the size of Lake Victoria, which supplies much of the Nile's water. Scientists worry that future droughts could also reduce the size of Lake Nasser, therefore reducing Egypt's water supply.

Scientists are not sure what the future will bring for the Nile. Global warming—rising temperatures on Earth—might bring more droughts to Africa and reduce the Nile's flow. On the other hand, heavy rains could end the droughts and keep the Nile's wondrous waters flowing far into the future.

3 Victoria Falls

Mist rising from Victoria Falls catches the colors of the sunset. The broad Zambezi River flows over the falls and into a deep, narrow channel at the bottom of a series of gorges.

$\mathcal{V}$ICTORIA FALLS IS A SPECTACULAR WATERFALL ON THE ZAMBEZI RIVER IN SOUTHERN AFRICA. AT THE FALLS, THE ZAMBEZI IS MORE THAN 1 MILE (1.6 KM) WIDE. THAT HUGE SHEET OF WATER PLUNGES OVER A CLIFF ABOUT 350 FEET (107 M) HIGH. VICTORIA FALLS IS ABOUT TWICE THE HEIGHT AND WIDTH OF NORTH AMERICA'S NIAGARA FALLS. THE GREAT WIDTH AND HEIGHT MAKE VICTORIA FALLS THE LARGEST SHEET OF FALLING WATER IN THE WORLD.

In earlier eras, people had different names for the falls. One local group called the falls Mosi-oa-Tunya, which means "smoke that thunders." The "smoke" was actually mist and spray from the waterfall. The roar of water tumbling over the falls sounded like thunder.

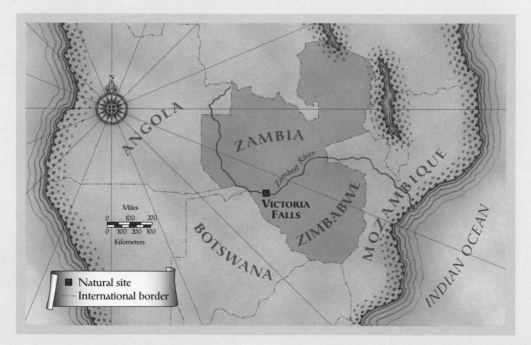

Local people believed that the area around the waterfall was a sacred place, where spirits lived. They believed that an evil god lived in the waterfall. To keep this god happy, people built statues and said prayers near the falls. They also buried their chiefs on an island near the falls.

The first European to see the falls was David Livingstone. Livingstone was a Scottish missionary. He spent more than thirty years in southern Africa. He explored the land and rivers. He also taught African people about the Christian religion and wrote books about his adventures.

David Livingstone was born in Scotland in 1813. He studied medicine as well as religion before his travels in Africa.

THE SMOKE *DID* THUNDER

In 1855 Livingstone was exploring the Zambezi River. He hoped it could become a watery highway from the Indian Ocean to the interior of Africa. Livingstone hoped that Europeans could sail up the Zambezi and trade with people in remote areas of Africa.

Paddling down the Zambezi in canoes, Livingstone and his local guides approached Mosi-oa-Tunya. They could see the "smoke" and hear the "thunder" almost 5 miles (8 km) away. The mist and spray rose up into the air in five huge columns—so tall that they seemed to mingle with the clouds.

"No one can imagine the beauty of the view from any thing witnessed in England. It had never been seen before by European eyes; but scenes so lovely must have been gazed upon by angels in their flight."

—David Livingstone, describing Victoria Falls, 1857

Rainbows and Moonbows

On sunny days, rainbows form in the spray above Victoria Falls. Sunlight shining through the water makes the rainbows appear. On nights when the moon is full and the sky is clear, "moonbows" appear in the spray. A moonbow is like a rainbow, except it's caused by moonlight, not sunlight. The moonbows above Victoria Falls sometimes extend from the top of the column of mist into the bottom of the falls.

A double rainbow forms over Victoria Falls.

Livingstone gave the falls a new name, Victoria Falls. That name honored Queen Victoria, who ruled Great Britain at the time. Livingstone later said that the falls were the most wonderful sight he had witnessed in thirty years in Africa.

GOING WITH THE FLOW

The Zambezi River begins in Zambia. It loops through Angola and back into Zambia. It then forms the border between Zambia and Zimbabwe. Victoria Falls is located on this border. After leaving Zambia and Zimbabwe, the Zambezi flows through Mozambique. It empties into the Indian Ocean. In total, it flows for about 1,600 miles (2,574 km).

Much of southern Africa has a rainy season from late November to early April and a dry season the rest of the year. During the rainy season, water runs off the land and flows into the Zambezi. This flood of water swells the river, making it larger, deeper, and swifter. Victoria Falls reaches its greatest size during this period. Spray from the falls rises hundreds of feet into the air. When the dry season sets in, the Zambezi shrinks. Victoria Falls takes on a calmer appearance. The column of mist shrinks and sometimes disappears.

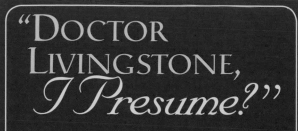

"DOCTOR LIVINGSTONE, I Presume?"

While exploring Africa, David Livingstone lost contact with the outside world for several years. Livingstone was famous in Europe and the United States. People there wondered what had happened to him. A newspaper, the *New York Herald*, sent a reporter to find Livingstone. The reporter was Henry Morton Stanley *(below)*. In 1871 Stanley found Livingstone in modern-day Tanzania. He greeted Livingstone with words that became world famous: "Dr. Livingstone, I presume?" People still use that phrase as a joke greeting.

Several islands sit near the crest, or edge, of the falls. One of them is Livingstone Island, named for David Livingstone. The islands divide the Zambezi's flow into smaller streams, which tumble over the falls separately. When the Zambezi is at its deepest, some of the islands disappear underwater. Only Livingstone and another large island remain exposed and divide the river into streams. During the dry season, the other islands reappear above the river's surface. Again, they create many small curtains of water.

Right: *When the river water is low, rocks and islands at the edge of the cliff divide Victoria Falls into many small waterfalls.*
Below: *The Zambezi River curves around a series of islands before reaching the falls.*

FORMING A FALLS

Geologists think that Victoria Falls began to form about 150 million years ago. In that era, one section of the Zambezi River flowed across gigantic cracks in the ground. The rock around the cracks was soft. The mighty Zambezi eroded, or wore away, the soft rock. The cracks got deeper and deeper. Eventually, they formed a deep gorge. The Zambezi tumbled over the edge of the gorge. This tumbling water was the beginning of Victoria Falls.

Over millions of years, the tumbling water eroded more rock along the edges of the river and at the bottom of the waterfall. The erosion made Victoria Falls wider and taller. The erosion continues, wearing rock away from the crest of the falls. As the rock disappears, the entire waterfall slowly moves back upstream along the Zambezi River.

A SHARED *Wonder*

Because Victoria Falls is located between Zambia and Zimbabwe, each of those countries controls half the falls.

This dramatic overhead photograph shows how the wide Zambezi tumbles into a narrow gorge.

BOILING *Pot*

At one place beneath the falls is a huge pool of water called the Boiling Pot. It swirls and foams like a boiling kettle of water. Sometimes, crocodiles, hippos, and other animals are swept over the falls and killed. People can sometimes see the dead animals swirling around in the pot.

WORRIES ABOUT THE WONDER

In the mid-1900s, Zambia and Zimbabwe established national parks at Victoria Falls. Park officials try to preserve the natural beauty of the falls. They decide whether people can build roads, hotels, and other buildings near the falls.

In modern times, Victoria Falls is one of Africa's most popular tourist attractions. More than three hundred thousand people visit the falls each year. Visitors also flock to the area for a chance to see elephants, hippopotamuses, white rhinos, and a variety of other wildlife. Visitors can walk very close to the falls, close enough to get soaking wet from the spray. They can take nature hikes to see the wild animals that live nearby.

Victoria Falls has been a UNESCO World Heritage Site since 1989. However, in 2007 UNESCO threatened to remove Victoria Falls from its World Heritage list. UNESCO leaders said that Zambian and Zimbabwean officials planned to build too many hotels, restaurants, and other tourist buildings near the falls. Those buildings could damage the natural beauty of the falls and the surrounding area.

People all over the world hope that Victoria Falls will not become too crowded with buildings. They hope that "the smoke that thunders" will continue to amaze future generations.

"A truly magnificent sight, and one which brings home the tremendous glory of the whole mighty work of Nature, and the comparative insignificance of Humanity."
— *British photographer P. M. Clarke, describing Victoria Falls, 1925*

4 THE Sahara Desert

Sand hills tower over palm trees at an oasis in the Sahara Desert. Sand hills are one of the many kinds of terrain in this vast, dry region.

ON SEPTEMBER 13, 1922, A WEATHER STATION RECORDED THE HOTTEST AIR TEMPERATURE EVER FOUND ON EARTH. IT WAS 136.4°F (58°C). WATER AT THAT TEMPERATURE IS DANGEROUSLY HOT. IT CAN BURN A PERSON'S SKIN IN ABOUT TEN SECONDS. THE SCORCHING TEMPERATURE WAS RECORDED IN THE SAHARA DESERT IN NORTHERN AFRICA. THE SAHARA IS THE WORLD'S BIGGEST HOT DESERT. IT COVERS AN AREA OF 3.5 MILLION SQUARE MILES (9.1 MILLION SQ. KM). THAT'S ABOUT THE SIZE OF THE UNITED STATES.

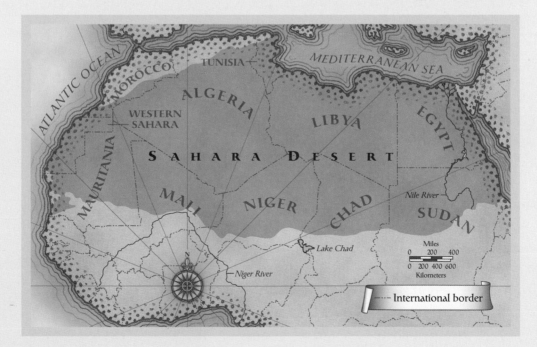

Rock formations rise above stony ground in the Libyan Desert, a Saharan region covering parts of Libya, Egypt, and Sudan. One of the driest places on Earth, this region includes not only areas of shifting sand dunes but also rocky plains with very little sand.

The record-breaking temperature reading came from a weather station in the nation of Libya. Weather stations record air temperature with a thermometer placed inside a shelter and shaded from the sun. If the temperature in the shade was that high, imagine how hot the Sahara must have been in the direct sunlight.

Some meteorologists (people who study the weather) think that temperatures in other parts of the Sahara may have been even higher that day. And the temperature of rocks on the desert floor on that day was probably above 170°F (77°C). At that temperature, you could almost fry an egg on a smooth rock.

EVER *Wonder?*

Has any place on Earth come close to the Sahara's record high temperature of 136.4°F (58°C)? Yes. On July 10, 1913, a weather station in Death Valley in California registered a temperature almost as hot as the Sahara's record. It was 134°F (57°C).

"The wind from the [Sahara] Desert is coming with a vengeance. Its breath is the pure flame of the furnace. . . . I had not the least idea that it could be so hot here in the middle of May. At 2 P.M., the thermometer in the sun was at 142° Fahrenheit [61°C]."

—British explorer James Richardson, 1845

On average, temperatures in the Sahara are about 86°F (30°C). But summer temperatures often rise above 122°F (50°C). Despite hot days, the Sahara chills out quickly after sunset. The Sahara is almost always cloudless. Clouds act like a nighttime blanket to keep heat near the land. Without clouds, heat from the Sahara escapes into space at night. Temperatures in the Sahara can fall below freezing (32°F, or 0°C) after dark.

Stars shine over the Sahara near Fezzan, Libya. Without clouds or vegetation to hold heat, the desert cools quickly at night.

D STANDS FOR DRY

Some people think that all deserts are hot places. But a place doesn't have to be hot to be a desert. It only has to be dry. Most scientists define deserts as places with less than 10 inches (25 cm) of rain per year.

The Sahara receives less than 3 inches (8 cm) of rain each year. By comparison, some rain forests get 200 inches (508 centimeters) of rain each year. The city of Chicago, Illinois, receives about 33 inches (84 cm) of yearly precipitation (rain and snow).

Heavy rains carved out this wadi (riverbed) in Morocco. Wadis usually are found in hilly areas of the desert.

When rain does fall in the Sahara, it pours. Heavy rain fills wadis, which are normally dry riverbeds. For a short time, the wadis flow like roaring rivers. People and animals sometimes drown in the quickly rising water. After a few hours, the rain ends. It may not rain again for an entire year.

THE "DESERT DESERT"

The name *Sahara* comes from an Arabic word that means "desert." So Sahara Desert really means "desert desert." The Sahara is one of three big deserts in Africa. The other two are the Kalahari Desert in southern Africa and the Namib Desert on the western coast of Namibia.

The Sahara makes up about 25 percent of the continent of Africa. It begins at the Mediterranean Sea and runs south for about 1,200 miles (1,930 km) into central Africa. East to west, it extends across the entire continent for more than 3,000 miles (4,830 km). It stretches from the Atlantic

DESERT *Facts*

Deserts cover about 20 percent of Earth's surface.

The word *desert* comes from the Latin word *desertum*. It means "to leave or abandon a place." This meaning makes sense, since deserts are usually too dry for people to live there.

The world's driest hot desert is the Atacama Desert in Chile. It gets almost ten times *less* rain than the Sahara.

DESERT Divider

Ocean in the west to the Red Sea in the east. It covers all or part of the African nations of Egypt, Libya, Algeria, Morocco, Mauritania, Mali, Niger, Chad, Sudan, and Tunisia.

Scientists think that this part of Africa was once wetter than it is in modern times. It was covered with grass and low shrubs. About four thousand years ago, the area started to get drier and hotter. After about three hundred years, it turned into a desert. Scientists are not certain why the change happened.

Strong winds shape the Great Sand Sea in the Sahara in Egypt. A large area of sand hills with little to no vegetation is called an erg. Smaller areas are called dune fields. The shifting sands make travel difficult.

"For there is no visible road or track in these parts [the Sahara], nothing but sand blown hither and thither by the wind. You see hills of sand in one place, and afterwards you will see them moved to quite another place."

—*Arab traveler and writer Ibn Battuta, 1300s*

SEAS OF SAND

About 80 percent of the Sahara has a flat, rocky surface, covered by small stones and gravel. The landscape also includes rocky hills and some mountains standing more than 11,000 feet (3,350 m) high.

Sand covers about 20 percent of the Sahara. In some places, "seas of sand" stretch as far as the eye can see. Strong desert winds sometimes blow the sand into big piles called dunes. The Sahara has the world's highest sand dunes. Some dunes are as high as an eighty-story skyscraper.

Sahara winds sometimes blow sand and dust through the air, creating fierce sandstorms. Sandstorms can be dangerous. People caught in a sandstorm might not be able to see their own hands in front of their faces. They can easily get lost. The sand can choke their lungs, hurt their eyes, and scrape their skin.

A section of the Sahara called the Ténéré covers most of Niger and part of Algeria. It includes both rocky hills and sand dunes.

A Malian man walks through a Saharan sandstorm near Timbuktu. Sandstorms can spring up with no warning, lasting from a few minutes to several days at a time. Desert travelers carry scarves or masks to protect their eyes and lungs during sudden storms.

LIFE IN THE DESERT

The Sahara has few permanent sources of freshwater. Only one big river—the Nile—runs through the Sahara. The Niger River runs southwest of the Sahara. A big lake, Lake Chad, sits at the southern edge of the desert.

The Sahara also has some oases. Oases are places in the desert where water flows to the surface through springs or wells. People who live near oases can grow fruits, vegetables, grain, and other crops.

Water in oases comes from aquifers. These underground layers of sand and gravel are soaked with water. The aquifers underneath the Sahara filled up with water thousands of years ago, when the land was wetter.

In ancient times, traders traveled with camels across the Sahara. They walked from one oasis to another. At oases, traders found freshwater and food. They could rest in the shade of palm trees.

In modern times, very few people live in the Sahara. Some desert dwellers tend herds of goats or cattle. These people move constantly,

The Mandara lakes are a group of saline (salty) lakes at the Ubari chain of oases in Libya. The lakes and freshwater wells support several villages where travelers and traders can rest and do business.

searching for fresh grass and water for their animals. A few farmers and fishers also live in or near the desert. Farmers live in villages near oases. Fishers live near rivers or on the shores of Lake Chad.

A variety of plants and animals live in the Sahara. These living things are suited to life in hot, dry weather. For instance, many of the Sahara's plants have waxy coatings on their leaves. These coatings help the plants conserve water. Desert animals, such as hares, lizards, and snakes, know how to protect themselves from the heat. They stay in underground burrows or under rocks during the scorching hot daytime. At night they come out to find food.

WORRIES ABOUT THE WONDER

The biggest worry about the Sahara is that it is growing. It is expanding southward by almost 2,000 feet (610 m) each year. The process is called

Niger's Tree of Ténéré was once a famous landmark in the Sahara. Drawing on water deep below the surface, it was the only tree for about 250 miles (402 km) in any direction. In 1973 a driver crashed his car into the tree and snapped its trunk.

DESERTS
without Heat

Not all deserts are hot. In fact, some deserts are freezing cold places covered by snow and ice. The world's biggest desert is on the continent of Antarctica. Temperatures in this frozen land may drop to –100°F (–73°C).

Antarctica might seem like a very wet place because of its thick covering of snow and ice—about 1 mile (1.6 km) thick in most places. Actually, Antarctica is very dry. In an average year, much of Antarctica gets less than 1 inch (2.5 cm) of precipitation. It took millions of years for Antarctica's thick covering of snow and ice to build up.

desertification. It happens when fertile lands dry up and become deserts.

Scientists think that human activity is one reason the Sahara is expanding. South of the desert, some people raise cattle for a living. Big herds of cattle eat a lot of grass. They eat it faster than new grass can grow. Once the grass is gone, the bare soil absorbs more heat from the sun. The land gets drier and hotter. Soil that once could grow grass becomes desert land. Scientists also worry that global warming could bring hotter, drier weather to lands near the Sahara.

When fertile lands turn into deserts, people can no longer make a living from the land. They can no longer grow crops or raise animals there. The growth of the Sahara has forced thousands of people to leave their farms and villages. They have moved to big cities to look for jobs.

People are trying to halt the growth of the Sahara. In some places, government workers have planted the desert soil with grasses and bushes that can withstand dry conditions. These new plants will help slow and stop desertification. Even though the Sahara is wondrous, this is one wonder that we don't want to get any bigger.

"I had entered [the Sahara] frivolously, like a fool. I left it as one stunned, crushed by the deadly majesty I had seen too closely."

—British explorer Hanns Vischer, 1906

5 MOUNT Kilimanjaro

Giraffes walk the grasslands at the foot of Mount Kilimanjaro. The peak is visible for many miles across the plains of Tanzania and Kenya.

$\mathcal{I}$N NORTHEASTERN TANZANIA, A MOUNTAIN PEAK GLITTERS IN THE SUN. IN EARLIER CENTURIES, LOCAL PEOPLE BELIEVED THE PEAK WAS SOLID SILVER. THEY THOUGHT THE MOUNTAINTOP'S INTERIOR CONTAINED SILVER AND DIAMONDS. ACCORDING TO LOCAL LEGENDS, EVIL SPIRITS AND DEMONS LIVED ON THE MOUNTAIN AND GUARDED THIS RICH TREASURE. THE LEGENDS SAID THAT PEOPLE WHO TRIED TO CLIMB THE MOUNTAIN SOMETIMES RETURNED WITH NO ARMS OR LEGS. SOMETIMES THEY NEVER RETURNED. THE FANTASTIC MOUNTAIN WAS MOUNT KILIMANJARO.

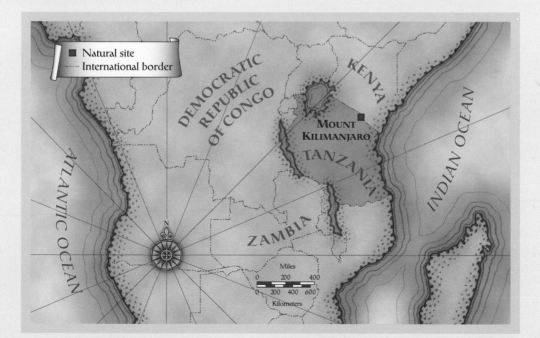

Mount Kilimanjaro is the world's highest freestanding mountain. Freestanding mountains are not part of a large mountain range or chain. They stand alone, without being connected to other mountains.

Mount Kilimanjaro is 19,341 feet (5,895 m) high. It rises out of the flat green savanna, or grasslands, of Tanzania in eastern Africa. No nearby mountains block the view. On clear days, people can see Mount Kilimanjaro from 125 miles (200 km) away.

Kilimanjaro is the highest mountain in Africa. Its snowcapped peak is a symbol of both Africa and of Tanzania. People have put pictures of the mountain on postage stamps, posters, and paper money. People sometimes call Kilimanjaro the Crown of Africa (because of its jewel-like peak) or the Roof of Africa (because it is so tall).

EVEN *Higher*

Many mountains are higher than Kilimanjaro. Mount Everest, for instance, is 29,028 feet (8,848 m) high. It is the highest mountain on Earth. Unlike Kilimanjaro, Mount Everest is not freestanding. It is part of the Himalaya mountain chain. The Himalayas contain more than one hundred mountains. The chain extends through Asia for 1,550 miles (2,500 km).

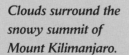

Clouds surround the snowy summit of Mount Kilimanjaro.

SNOW, NOT SILVER

For centuries, only local people knew about Kilimanjaro. While working in Africa in the 1840s, German missionary Johannes Rebmann heard about the mountain. He set out to find it. Ignoring local warnings about evil spirits, Rebmann hired local guides to take him to the mountain. He arrived in April, becoming the first person from outside Africa to see Mount Kilimanjaro.

Rebmann didn't believe that Kilimanjaro was capped with silver. He thought that snow and ice on top of the mountain caused it to glitter in the sunlight. Rebmann did not climb the mountain. But he wrote an article about it for a missionary magazine. After the story appeared, news of the enormous snowcapped mountain quickly spread around the world.

At first, some people didn't believe Rebmann's story. Mount Kilimanjaro is located 211 miles (340 km) south of the equator. That imaginary line divides Earth into a northern half and a southern half. Most areas near the equator are hot and humid year-round. Some people didn't understand how a mountain near the equator could be covered with snow and ice. They didn't realize that

"This morning we [saw Mount Kilimanjaro] more distinctly than ever. . . . I fancied I saw a dazzlingly white cloud. My Guide called the white which I saw merely 'Beredi,' [meaning] 'cold.' It was perfectly clear to me, however, that it could be nothing else but 'snow.'"

— *missionary Johannes Rebmann, 1848*

even near the equator, mountaintops are extremely cold.

Soon other missionaries and explorers visited Mount Kilimanjaro. Adventurers began to climb the mountain, hoping to be the first one to the top. As people climbed higher and higher, they discovered that the mountain was indeed covered with ice and snow. In 1889 German geographer Hans Meyer reached the top of Kibo, Kilimanjaro's highest peak.

A SLEEPING VOLCANO

Many mountaintops have narrow, pointed peaks. Some mountain peaks are so narrow that only one or two people can stand on the very top at one time. The top of Mount Kilimanjaro is different. Instead of peaks, it has bowl-shaped craters, or hollows, on top. The biggest crater is almost 1.5 miles (2.4 km) wide. Eight high school football fields, placed end to end, could fit inside the crater.

What created the craters? Mount Kilimanjaro is made up of volcanoes. A volcano is an opening in Earth's surface. Occasionally, melted rock, hot ash, and hot gases from deep inside Earth erupt through the opening. Afterward, the rock and ashes cool, harden, and pile up around the opening.

The setting sun sparkles on the peak of Mount Kilimanjaro as the moon rises above.

WHAT'S IN A *Name?*

Nobody is certain how Mount Kilimanjaro got its name. The name might come from *kilima njaro*. This term means "shining mountain" in Swahili, one of the languages of Tanzania.

SMOKING *Brothers*

The Chagga people moved into the fertile area around Mount Kilimanjaro about three hundred years ago. The Chagga tell stories about smoke and fire on top of the mountain. According to one legend, the summits Kibo and Mawenzi are brothers. The legend says that one day, Kibo lit Mawenzi's pipe. Perhaps the story means that at first, smoke and lava (red-hot rock) were pouring from Kibo and then they began pouring from Mawenzi.

After many eruptions, the hardened materials create a cone-shaped mountain around the volcano. A crater forms in the center of the volcano, where the hot materials blast through to the sky.

Kilimanjaro has three summits: Kibo, Shira, and Mawenzi. Each of these summits is a volcano. Scientists believe that Shira and Mawenzi are extinct volcanoes, meaning that they probably will not erupt again. Kibo, however, is an active volcano and may erupt in the future. Scientists think that a pool of melted rock sits just 1,300 feet (400 m) below the

Kibo's volcanic crater is visible at times of low snow cover.

Above: *A Tanzanian woman weeds a coffee field below Mount Kilimanjaro.* Left: *In 2002 the Nyiragongo Volcano in the Democratic Republic of Congo erupted, killing dozens of people and driving three hundred thousand from their homes.*

earth beneath Kibo. Nobody knows when Kibo last erupted. Some scientists think it has been inactive for about a hundred thousand years ago. But local people say that the mountain erupted more recently.

Volcanoes can be very destructive. They spew out hot ash, rock, and gases that can burn buildings and hurt plants, animals, and people living nearby. But volcanoes also provide benefits. After they cool, ash and rock from volcanoes turn into a thick layer of fertile soil. This soil is good for growing crops. People living near Mount Kilimanjaro grow abundant crops of corn, beans, yams, bananas, coffee, and other foods.

"What words can adequately describe this glimpse of majestic grandeur and godlike repose?"
—Scottish explorer Joseph Thomson, 1883

Snow covers ridges at the summit of Mount Kilimanjaro. Warming temperatures on Earth have caused some of the snow and ice to melt in recent years.

WORRIES ABOUT THE WONDER

To protect and preserve this natural wonder, Tanzania's government opened Kilimanjaro National Park in 1977. The park includes the mountains and surrounding forests. According to park rules, people are not allowed to cut trees around the mountain. In 1987 UNESCO declared Kilimanjaro National Park to be a World Heritage Site.

Global warming is one of the most serious threats to Mount Kilimanjaro. As Earth's climate has warmed, the ice sheets that give Kilimanjaro its silvery top have begun melting and getting smaller. Some scientists think the ice sheets could disappear completely by the year 2015. Warmer weather could also bring drier weather to this part of Africa. Trees need plenty of water to live and grow. Dry weather could kill trees and damage forests around the mountain.

But Kilimanjaro would experience much worse damage if Kibo erupted again. An explosive eruption could blow away part of the mountain. An eruption could also make Kilimanjaro's top collapse and fall in upon itself. Kilimanjaro would become smaller and shorter.

Of course, nobody knows if Kibo will erupt or how it would change Kilimanjaro if it did. This natural wonder may well remain just as wonderful long into the future.

CLIMBING *Kilimanjaro*

Each year about twenty-five thousand people try to climb Mount Kilimanjaro. The climb takes almost a week. High up on the mountain, climbers must cope with thin air, or air that is low in oxygen. Breathing becomes difficult. The weather also gets quite cold high on the mountain. Many people turn back before reaching the top. But every year, several thousand climbers make it to the top.

Hi, *Mom!*

It's possible to call home from the top of Mount Kilimanjaro. The mountaintop has cell phone service. Climbers can also call home from the top of Mount Everest and other tall mountains.

Above: *Climbers make their way up the side of Mount Kilimanjaro. It takes six to eight days of hiking to reach the summit.* Below: *Shrinking snow fields expose bare rock at Uhuru peak on Mount Kilimanjaro.*

6 The Seychelles ISLANDS

Waves wash against the white sand of Grand Anse Beach on La Digue Island in the Seychelles Islands. The islands are known for their tropical beauty and fascinating plants and animals.

*I*N THE 1500s, EUROPEAN SAILORS IN THE INDIAN OCEAN, OFF THE EAST COAST OF AFRICA, SOMETIMES SAW MYSTERIOUS OBJECTS FLOATING IN THE WATER. SOMETIMES SAILORS PADDLED OUT IN ROWBOATS TO SNARE THE OBJECTS AND BRING THEM BACK ON BOARD THEIR SHIPS. OTHER SAILORS RUSHED ONTO THE DECK, PUSHING AND SHOVING TO GET A LOOK.

The objects were huge seeds, almost twice as big as basketballs. Some sailors thought the seeds were the "forbidden fruit" mentioned in the story of Adam and Eve in the Bible. They thought that the delightful Garden of Eden (Adam and Eve's home) must be somewhere nearby. Other sailors believed that the seeds grew on palm trees rooted on the bottom of the ocean. They called the seeds *coco-de-mer,* which means "coconut of the sea."

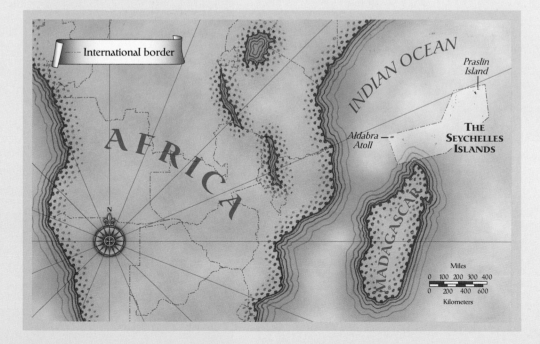

Left: *Giant seeds cluster at the top of a coco-de-mer palm tree.* Below: *The coco-de-mer palm seed's unusual shape has brought it a lot of attention.*

In fact, the seeds did come from palm trees. But the trees grew on land, not in the water. The trees grew on the Seychelles Islands, a group of about one hundred small islands in the Indian Ocean. The trees—coco-de-mer palms—were part of a world of astonishing plants and animals found nowhere else on Earth.

Like the biblical Garden of Eden, the Seychelles are a rare paradise on Earth. The islands have breathtaking beauty. They have year-round warm weather, white beaches, blue skies, swaying palm trees, and a clean, peaceful environment.

A BIG BREAKUP

About half of the islands of the Seychelles are made of a hard substance called coral.

EVER *Wonder?*

If coco-de-mer palm seeds float in the ocean, why don't they grow in other places besides the Seychelles? Coco-de-mer palms grow only where fresh seeds fall to the ground. Fresh seeds are too heavy to float in the water. The seeds that sometimes float in the ocean are already dried out. They have rotted and died. Only the outer husk remains. Even if these seeds landed in new places, they could not grow into new trees.

Coral comes from the skeletons of dead sea creatures, which are also called corals. The other half of the islands of the Seychelles are made of granite. The granite islands are the oldest ocean islands on Earth. They formed hundreds of millions of years ago.

Scientists think that, about 300 million years ago, Earth contained a single landmass named Pangaea. About 200 million years ago, this supercontinent broke up into two chunks—Laurasia in the north and Gondwanaland in the south. About 170 million years ago, these two landmasses broke into smaller pieces to form our modern continents. Laurasia became Europe, Asia, and North America. Gondwanaland became Australia, South America, Africa, India, and Antarctica.

The granite islands of the Seychelles are scraps of granite left over from Gondwanaland's breakup. Their rock formed more than 700 million years ago, before Pangaea even existed.

Praslin Island is the second-largest island in the Seychelles. It is a granite island with a mountainous interior. The island also has many popular beaches and scuba diving sites.

> *"These [islands] seemed to us an earthly Paradise."*
> —*English sailor Thomas Jones, 1609*

PARADISE FOUND

For millions of years, the Seychelles had no contact with the rest of the world. Many of the plants and animals that lived there were unchanged from the time of Gondwanaland. For millions of years, no people lived on the Seychelles.

In the early centuries A.D., Arab traders probably passed the Seychelles on voyages across the Indian Ocean. Portuguese explorer Vasco da Gama saw the islands in 1502, during a voyage to India. English sailors landed on the Seychelles in 1609. They established a base where English ships could stock up on food and water. French explorers claimed the islands as French territory in 1756. The French named the islands after Jean Moreau de Séchelles, a French government official.

LONG-LIVED GIANTS

When people arrived in the Seychelles, they quickly discovered the islands' amazing plants and animals. The coco-de-mer palm is one of the most interesting plants. It grows only in a forest in the Vallée de Mai (Valley of May), a secluded valley on Praslin Island.

Coco-de-mer palms can live for two hundred to four hundred years. Their tall slender trunks may tower to a height of 100 feet (31 m), almost as high as a ten-story building. At the top of the trunk grows a fan-shaped cluster of leaves. These are the biggest leaves of any plant on Earth. They can measure 33 feet (10 m) long and 15 feet (4.5 m) wide.

Portuguese explorer Vasco da Gama made three trips to India before his death in 1524. This portrait of da Gama appears in a manuscript created in 1646.

"The original home of the coco de mer, the Seychelles, is a [true] Garden of Eden."

—New York Times, *1906*

A waterfall pours between coco-de-mer palms inside the Vallée de Mai Nature Reserve on Praslin Island. Visitors to the park can walk beneath giant leaves in a palm forest almost untouched by human beings.

The seed of the coco-de-mer palm is the largest seed in the world. It can weigh more than 40 pounds (18 kg). The seed has two rounded sections with a groove between them. It looks a lot like the rear end of a human being—which is one reason the early European sailors were so curious about them.

GIANTS AND DWARFS

Amazing animals also live on the Seychelles—both on land and in the water. For instance, the pygmy piping frog is one of the world's smallest animals. When fully grown, it is only as big as a person's fingernail. Giant tortoises weighing up to 600 pounds (273 kg) also live on the Seychelles. A colony of more than 150,000 tortoises lives on Aldabra Atoll, a group of four coral islands.

Lurking below the water is the world's largest shark. Called the whale shark, it is almost the size of a school bus. This giant grows up to 40 feet (12 m) long and may weigh 30,000 pounds (14,000 kg). It eats small plants and animals floating in the sea.

Some of the rarest birds in the world fly through the air over the Seychelles. One of them is the Seychelles

Inset: *The pygmy piping frog gets its name from its tiny size and its squeaky call.* Below: *The Syechelles magpie robin* (left) *is very rare, while the Seychelles giant tortoise* (right) *is found in greater numbers.*

In earlier centuries, pirates who had raided merchant ships along the African coast sometimes stopped in the Seychelles. Legends say that fabulous treasures of gold, silver, and jewels from sunken pirate ships are still buried there.

magpie robin. These birds have shiny, coal-black feathers with a bright white stripe across each wing. Magpie robins were abundant on the Seychelles until people arrived. With the people came rats and pet cats that killed many magpie robins. By the early 2000s, only about one hundred of the birds remained alive. Another rare bird is the black parrot. About two hundred black parrots live on the Seychelles.

WORRIES ABOUT THE WONDER

In the 2000s, thousands of tourists visit the Seychelles Islands each year. They come to see coco-de-mer palms, rare birds, giant tortoises, and the other natural wonders. The tourists help the Seychelles by spending their money. The tourist industry provides jobs for local people in hotels, restaurants, and other businesses.

The government of the Seychelles wants to make sure that tourists don't hurt the islands' plants and animals. The government has established national parks and preserves to protect wildlife. Vallée de Mai and its palm forest, for instance, are part of a national park. Park rules prevent visitors from collecting coco-de-mar seeds, picking plants, and interfering with animals.

UNESCO recognizes the importance of the Seychelles and the need to protect this natural wonder. It has selected two places in the Seychelles as World Heritage Sites. One is the Vallée de Mai. The other is the Aldabra Atoll, home to the colony of giant tortoises.

"The Vallée de Mai is an outstanding reminder of what the world's [plant life] was like at an earlier stage, a kind of living museum."

—UNESCO, 1994

7
THE
Serengeti Plain

Migrating animals crowd the plains of the Serengeti National Park in Tanzania. Millions of animals make the journey across the Serengeti Plain each year.

$\mathcal{T}$HE SERENGETI PLAIN OF NORTHERN TANZANIA PROVIDES A STAGE FOR ONE OF THE GREATEST ANIMAL SHOWS ON EARTH. THE SHOW IS AN ANIMAL MIGRATION THAT HAS BEEN PLAYING FOR ALMOST ONE MILLION YEARS. AN ANIMAL MIGRATION IS A REGULAR MOVEMENT OF ANIMALS FROM ONE PLACE TO ANOTHER.

Animals often migrate to find food or better weather. For instance, some birds in North America fly south every winter. They escape the cold weather. They fly to places where food is more abundant. In the spring, when it warms up in the north, the birds migrate back to build nests and lay eggs.

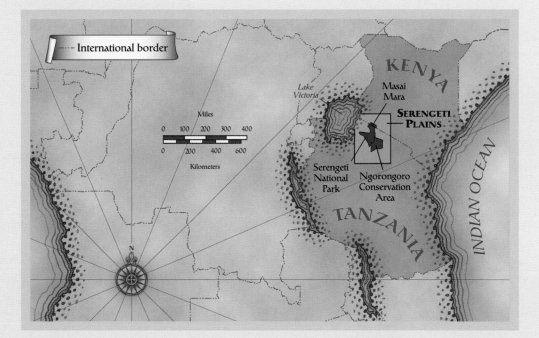

On the Serengeti Plain, about two million animals undertake a yearly migration. More than half the animals are large antelopes called wildebeests. The other animals are zebras and Thomson's gazelles (also a kind of antelope).

The name Serengeti comes from *siringitu*. In the language of the local Masai people, *siringitu* means "endless plains." Indeed, the Serengeti does seem endless. This vast flatland is about the size of the U.S. state of New Jersey. In addition to the antelopes and zebras, the Serengeti is home to elephants, rhinoceroses, crocodiles, cheetahs, lions, and many other animals.

HOOFING IN A CIRCLE

The Serengeti migration begins in Kenya, north of Tanzania, in a place called the Masai Mara. There, in September and October, the animals feed on tall grasses. In November the dry season sets in on the Masai Mara. Ponds and creeks dry up. Grass stops growing. It turns the color of toast and crackles underfoot. The animals soon run out of food.

As the Masai Mara dries up, rains begin to fall in the southern part of the Serengeti. The lands there become lush and green. The animals head south to feed on the newly grown grasses.

ODD *Birds*

Some unusual birds live on the Serengeti. Bee-eaters are birds that gobble down bees and wasps. Before eating the insects, bee-eaters bang them on hard surfaces to remove their stingers. Secretary birds *(below)* have tufts of feathers that stick up from the top of their heads.

"*The abundance of [wild animals] was really magnificent. Large herds of antelope roamed around and long-maned gnus, light footed zebras and, singly or in pairs, the broad backs of rhinos.*"

— *Austrian geographer Oscar Baumann, 1882*

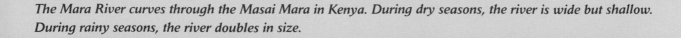

"We walked for miles over burnt out country. . . .
Then I saw the green trees of the river, walked two
miles [3 km] more and found myself in paradise."
—hunter Stewart Edward White, 1913

The Mara River curves through the Masai Mara in Kenya. During dry seasons, the river is wide but shallow. During rainy seasons, the river doubles in size.

Above: *A herd of gnus crosses the Mara River in Tanzania.* Right: *Migrating animals leave permanent paths across the Serengeti Plain.*

They stop to graze until all the grass in one place has been eaten. Then they move on.

In a pattern that's repeated year after year, the animals follow the rains to fresh grasslands. The pattern of rainfall takes them in a clockwise direction. In the course of the year, they travel in a 500-mile (804 km) circle. By September the animals are back where they started, in the Masai Mara.

ENDLESS ANIMALS

When the animals are on the move, they cover the Serengeti Plain as far as the eye can see. Sounds from the animals fill the air—the bleating cry of wildebeests and the yelping bark of zebras. As the animals travel, their hooves kick up clouds of dust.

When the migration begins, some of the animals are old, weak, and sick. These animals may have a difficult journey. They sometimes have to walk for days without food until they reach areas with fresh grass. They must struggle across rivers, where hungry crocodiles wait for a tasty meal.

Scientists estimate that hundreds of thousands of animals die during the yearly migration. Some die from starvation, illness, or injuries. Others are killed by lions, cheetahs, hyenas, crocodiles, or wild dogs. For those predators, the migration is an all-you-can-eat buffet. The predators target their attacks on animals that are old, sick, or injured. The migration also provides meals for vultures, storks, and other animals that feed on the bodies of dead animals.

A cheetah brings down an injured Thomson's gazelle in the Masai Mara National Reserve in Kenya. Cheetahs prey on smaller animals, like gazelles, and on young zebras and wildebeests. When hunting, they depend on their ability to reach speeds of up to 75 miles (120 km) per hour to outrun their prey.

PEOPLE ON THE PLAIN

The Serengeti is one of the oldest ecosystems, or communities of living things, on Earth. Scientists think that the plain has existed in its present form for at least 1.6 million years. Its climate, plants, and animal life have not changed much over that time.

In addition to animals, the Serengeti Plain has long provided a home for human beings. In the 1950s, British archaeologists Louis and Mary Leakey started digging in Olduvai Gorge, a steep-sided valley in the eastern Serengeti. The Leakeys found skeletons, knives, and other tools of early humans who lived on the Serengeti Plain more than 2 million years ago. They found the skull of a being called *Homo habilis*, an early kind of human being. The discoveries at Olduvai Gorge showed that early humans were skilled toolmakers.

People called the Masai have lived on the Serengeti Plain for hundreds of years. In earlier centuries, the Masai made a living by herding cattle on the plain. They knew about the great migration of animals, but few outsiders knew about the migration.

Louis Leakey holds fossilized teeth that he and Mary Leakey excavated in Olduvai Gorge, Tanzania, in 1973.

A Masai man herds sheep on a farm in Kenya. For centuries the Masai moved their herds of cows, goats, and sheep around the Serengeti Plain to take advantage of seasonal rains.

A big-game hunter, accompanied by two Kenyan guides, claims the body of a black rhinoceros that he killed on the Serengeti around 1895. In 1900 the black rhinoceros was the most numerous of all rhinoceroses in Africa. By the end of the century, hunting had made it one of the rarest rhinos.

SHOOTING THE *Big Five*

In the early 1900s, hunters went to the Serengeti to shoot wild animals. Hunters often saved the heads of the animals they killed and hung them on the wall as trophies. Many hunters dreamed of shooting the Serengeti's most prized wild animals: lions, leopards, elephants, rhinoceroses, and African buffalo. Hunters called these animals the Big Five. Modern visitors to Serengeti National Park also dream of shooting the Big Five—with cameras!

In the late 1800s, hunters from Europe and the United States started to visit the Serengeti. In 1913 U.S. author and hunter Stewart Edward White visited the area. White wrote a book about his adventures. His descriptions of millions of wild animals amazed readers in North America and Europe. More writers, tourists, and scientists came to Tanzania to see the animals for themselves.

WORRIES ABOUT THE WONDER

In modern times, thousands of visitors come to the Serengeti Plain each year. Some visit Serengeti National Park, in the northern part of the plain. Others visit the Ngorongoro Conservation Area in the south.

Above: *Tourists on safari watch a herd of elephants in Tanzania. Safaris can last from a few hours of driving to more than two weeks of hiking and camping in the wild. Below: Zebras and wildebeests graze at the edge of the Mara River in Tanzania.*

Going on Safari

Many people who visit the Serengeti go on safari. In the Swahili language, that word means "journey." Years ago, safaris were trips through wild lands to hunt animals. A modern safari is a journey to see and photograph animals in the wild, without causing them any harm.

UNESCO listed the Ngorongoro Conservation Area as a World Heritage Site in 1979. The Serengeti National Park became a World Heritage Site in 1981.

Both parks have hotels and restaurants for tourists. Tour guides take visitors through the parks for close-up views of the animals. They travel in vehicles that can handle rugged terrain.

Hunting is forbidden in the parks. Rangers patrol the parks to enforce this rule. However, people living near the park sometimes break the law. Hunters illegally kill about two hundred thousand animals each year. Some animals, including elephants and rhinoceroses, have almost all disappeared from the parks because of illegal hunting. However, the Serengeti's spectacular animal migration continues year after year.

"[I saw] vast numbers of black and white specks that looked very much as salt and pepper. . . . I focused my [binoculars] and to my amazement the specks came to life and resolved themselves into enormous herds of wildebeest and zebras. The brightly marked zebras were the tiny grains of salt. The dark wildebeest were the flakes of pepper. . . . I could hardly believe my eyes, so vast were their numbers."

— U.S. scientist James Clark, 1909

TIMELINE

ca. 5000 B.C.   People begin to settle in villages along the northern Nile River in Egypt. These villages eventually become a great civilization.

400s B.C.   Herodotus makes a list of the Seven Wonders of the World. People made other lists of wonders, including lists of natural wonders.

A.D. 150   Ptolemy concludes that the Nile River begins in the Mountains of the Moon in central Africa.

1502   Portuguese explorer Vasco da Gama spots the Seychelles Islands.

1618   Pedro Páez discovers that a spring in Ethiopia is the the source of the Blue Nile.

1847   Thomas Staughton Savage writes the first description of gorillas. He chooses the name *gorilla* from an ancient Greek story.

1848   Johannes Rebmann becomes the first non-African to see Mount Kilimanjaro.

1855   David Livingstone becomes the first European to see Victoria Falls. He names the falls for Britain's Queen Victoria.

1864   John Speke determines that Lake Victoria is the ultimate source of the Nile River.

1889   Hans Meyer becomes the first climber to reach the top of Mount Kilimanjaro.

1922   The highest air temperature ever measured on Earth is recorded in the Sahara Desert.

1950s   Louis and Mary Leakey discover early human remains in Olduvai Gorge in the eastern Serengeti.

1960s   Egypt builds the Aswan High Dam on the Nile River. The dam keeps the river from flooding and also provides electricity and water for Egypt's people.

1967   Dian Fossey sets up a gorilla research center in the Virunga Mountains in Rwanda.

1979   Virunga National Park becomes a World Heritage Site. The Ngorongoro Conservation Area becomes a World Heritage Site.

1981   Serengeti National Park becomes a World Heritage Site.

1982   The Aldabra Atoll (island group) in the Seychelles becomes a World Heritage Site.

1983   Vallée de Mai becomes a World Heritage Site.

1985   Unknown killers murder Dian Fossey in Rwanda.

1987 Mount Kilimanjaro becomes a World Heritage Site.

1989 Victoria Falls becomes a World Heritage Site.

2007 A team of scientists claim that the Amazon River is longer than the Nile.

2008 Authorities arrest a park ranger for the 2007 killings of ten mountain gorillas in Virunga National Park.

CHOOSE AN EIGHTH WONDER

Now that you've read about the seven natural wonders of Africa, do a little research to choose an eighth wonder. You may enjoy working with a friend.

To do your research, look at some of the websites and books listed on pages 76 and 77. Look for places in Africa that
- *are especially large*
- *are exceptionally beautiful*
- *were unknown to foreigners for many centuries*
- *are unlike any other place on Earth*

You might even try gathering photos and writing your own chapter on the eighth wonder!

GLOSSARY AND PRONUNCIATION GUIDE

aquifer: a layer of rock, sand, or gravel that holds water close to Earth's surface

continents: the seven giant landmasses on Earth. The continents are Africa, Antarctica, Asia, Australia, Europe, North America, and South America.

desert: a dry land that receives less than 10 inches (25 cm) of rain or snow each year

drought: a period of little or no rainfall

ecosystem: a community of living and nonliving things (including plants, animals, rocks, and water) that interact with and depend on one another

erode: to wear away rock and soil. Wind, rain, rivers, and other natural processes are responsible for most erosion.

extinction: the complete dying out of a plant or animal species

geographer: a scientist who studies Earth's physical features and how they interact with plants and animals

global warming: an increase in Earth's average temperatures. Most scientists think that air pollution is causing global warming.

habitat: the place where a plant or animal normally lives and grows

migration: the regular movement of groups of animals from one place to another

oasis: a wet or green area in a desert

precipitation: rain or snowfall

predator: an animal that gets its food by attacking and eating other animals

volcano: an opening in Earth's surface through which melted rock and gases occasionally burst forth

Kilimanjaro: kih-luh-muhn-JAHR-oh

Masai: mah-SY

Nile: NYLE

Sahara: suh-HAR-uh

Serengeti: sehr-uhn-GEH-tee

Seychelles: say-SHEHLZ

Victoria: vihk-TAW-ree-ah

Virunga: vee-ROON-gah

Zambezi: zam-BEE-zee

SOURCE NOTES

13 George Beals Schaller, "Exploring the Environment: Mountain Gorillas," *Wheeling Jesuit University*, April 28, 2005, http://www.cotf.edu/ete/modules/mgorilla/mgeuropean .html (November 25, 2007).

17 Paul Halsall, "Hymn to the Nile," *Internet Ancient History Sourcebook*, 2008, http://www .fordham.edu/halsall/ancient/hymn-nile.html (November 4, 2007).

18 Archaeological Legacy Institute, "Egypt: Gift of the Nile," *Archaeology Channel*, 1992, http://www.archaeologychannel.org/content/video/Egyptgift.html (November 15, 2007).

19 Richard Bangs and Pasquale Scaturro, *Mystery of the Nile: The Epic Story of the First Descent of the World's Deadliest River* (New York: Penguin Group, 2005), 53.

26 David Livingstone, "Discovery of the Victoria Falls–1855," *Safari Company*, 2007, http://www.thesafaricompany.co.za/Articles_Livingstone_Discovers_Victoria_Falls.htm (May 17, 2008).

31 ZNTB, "The Victoria Falls," *Zambia National Tourist Board*, 2007, http://www .zambiatourism.com/travel/places/victoria.htm (November 2, 2007).

35 James Richardson, "Travels in the Great Desert of Sahara, in the Years of 1845 and 1846," *Project Gutenberg*, July 17, 2007, http://www.gutenberg.org/ files/22094/22094-0.txt (November 11, 2007).

38 Paul Halsall, "Ibn Battuta: Travels in Asia and Africa 1325–1354," *Medieval Sourcebook*, December 2006, http://www.fordham.edu/halsall/source/1354-ibnbattuta.html (April 8, 2008).

41 Alex Chadwick, "Sahara Trek," *National Public Radio*, December 20, 2002, http:// www.npr.org/programs/re/archivesdate/2002/dec/johnhare/index.html (November 7, 2007).

45 NTZ, "Kilimanjaro before 1900," *Northern Tanzania Information*, September 2007, http://www.ntz.info/gen/n01734.html (November 15, 2007).

49 Audrey Salkeld, *Kilimanjaro: To the Roof of Africa* (Washington, DC: National Geographic, 2002), 21.

56 Judith Skerrett, "Island Conservation—The First Glimpse of Seychelles," *News Headlines*, October 18, 2006, http://www.virtualseychelles.sc/news/news_details.asp?id=1038 (November 26, 2007).

57 R. W. Plant, "Most Famous of All Palms, the Coco de Mer," *New York Times*, January 28, 1906, SM7.

59 Guy Lionnet, "The Vallée de Mai: A Paradise Garden in the Seychelles Nature Reserve, *UNESCO Courier*, April 1994, http://findarticles.com/p/articles/mi_m1310/is_1994_ April/ai_15630629 (November 25, 2007).

62 Myles Turner, *My Serengeti Years: The Memoirs of an African Games Warden* (New York: W. W. Norton, 1988), 25.

63 Lota Melamari, "The Serengeti," *Absolute Adventure Travel*, 2004, http://www
    .absoluteadventuretravel.com/serengeti.htm (November 10, 2007).

69 Ibid., 26.

SELECTED BIBLIOGRAPHY

Allan, Tony, and Andrew Warren, eds. *Deserts: The Encroaching Wilderness*. New York:
    Oxford University Press, 1993.

Cleare, John. *Mountains of the World*. San Diego: Thunder Bay Press, 1997.

Collins, Mark, ed. *The Last Rain Forests: A World Conservation Atlas*. New York: Oxford
    University Press, 1990.

Flegg, Jim. *Deserts: Miracle of Life*. New York: Facts on File, 1993.

Hanbury-Tenison, Robin. *The Oxford Book of Exploration*. Oxford: Oxford University Press,
    1993.

Hancock, Paul, and Brian J. Skinner, eds. *The Oxford Companion to the Earth*. Oxford:
    Oxford University Press, 2000.

Langewiesche, William. *Sahara Unveiled: A Journey across the Desert*. New York: Pantheon
    Books, 1996.

Luhr, James F., ed. *Earth*. London: Dorling Kindersley, 2003.

Man, John, and Chris Schuler. *The Traveler's Atlas*. Hauppage, NY: Barron's Educational
    Services, 1998.

Ridgeway, Rick. *The Shadow of Kilimanjaro: On Foot across East Africa*. New York: Henry Holt,
    1998.

Salkeld, Audrey. *Kilimanjaro: To the Roof of Africa*. Washington, DC: National Geographic,
    2002.

FURTHER READING AND WEBSITES

Books

Alter, Judy. *Extraordinary Explorers and Adventurers*. New York: Children's Press, 2001. This book describes the adventures of David Livingstone, Henry Morton Stanley, and other explorers. Alter provides brief explanations of their motivations and triumphs.

Ayo, Yvonne. *Eyewitness: Africa*. New York: Dorling Kindersley, 2000. This richly illustrated book offers easy-to-understand information on Africa, including its cultures, customs, religions, and crafts.

Bangs, Richard, and Pasquale Scaturro. *Mystery of the Nile: The Epic Story of the First Descent of the World's Deadliest River*. New York: Penguin Group, 2005. Imagine traveling 3,000 miles (4,827 km) in 114 days and encountering crocodiles, people armed with automatic weapons, and sandstorms. This book describes an expedition to the Nile that did just that in 2004.

Bundy, Nikki. *Drought and the Earth*. Minneapolis: Lerner Publications Company, 2001. Drought is a serious threat to the people, plants, and animals of Africa. Droughts could cause the Sahara Desert to grow even larger. Find out all about droughts in this title for young readers.

Day, Nancy. Y*our Travel Guide to Ancient Egypt*. Minneapolis: Twenty-First Century Books, 2001. The Nile River gave life to ancient Egypt—one of the world's great ancient civilizations. Here, readers will learn about day-to-day life for ancient Egyptians.

DiPiazza, Francesca. *Zimbabwe in Pictures*. Minneapolis: Twenty-First Century Books, 2005. Victoria Falls sits on Zimbabwe's northern border. This book explores Zimbabwe's other natural wonders, as well as its history, people, and culture.

Jackson, Tom. *Animals of Africa and Europe*. London: Southwater, 2004. This book explores a breathtaking collection of huge and tiny mammals, amphibians, and reptiles from these two continents. The photographs present the animals in their natural habitats.

Moore, Robert J., Jr. *Natural Wonders of the World*. New York: Abbeville Press, 2000. Gorgeous photographs accompany this informative text about fifty natural wonders. Each continent is represented, with explanations about each one's geology, geography, and plant and animal life.

Palin, Michael. *Sahara*. New York: St. Martin's Press, 2002. Michael Palin relates the story of his trip across Africa—from Algeria through the Atlas Mountains of Morocco and into the Sahara Desert. He writes about the numerous cultures he encountered along the way.

Roe-Pimm, Nancy. *The Heart of the Beast: Eight Great Gorilla Stories*. Minneapolis: Darby Creek Publishing, 2007. Through interviews with experts and even gorillas themselves, this book offers new insights into these once-misunderstood animals.

Woods, Michael, and Mary B. Woods. *Volcanoes*. Minneapolis: Lerner Publications Company, 2007. The Woodses provide an explanation of how volcanoes such as Mount Kilimanjaro have altered the face of Earth.

Websites

African Animals—Serengeti, Ngorongoro and Lake Manyara

http://www.iserengeti.com/african-animals.html

Click on the name of an animal to find pictures and information. The site includes many links and a map showing where animals live in Africa.

Ancient Egypt: Life along the Nile

http://www.beyondbooks.com/wcu81/3a.asp

This site offers a clear overview of life in ancient Egypt. Visitors can find out about native animals, hear an ancient Egyptian hymn, view maps, and more.

Animals: Creature Feature

http://kids.nationalgeographic.com/Animals/CreatureFeature/Mountain-gorilla

Visitors to this site can watch mountain gorillas playing, interacting with their families, and moving through their natural terrain.

The Story of Africa: African History from the Dawn of Time

http://www.bbc.co.uk/worldservice/africa/features/storyofafrica/

At this site, African historians write about their continent and its people. The site explains the oral traditions that have kept African history and myths alive for future generations.

Visual Geography Series

http://www.vgsbooks.com

Visitors to this site can find links to more information about the countries that are home to Africa's natural wonders. Read about the land, history, government, people, culture, and economy of Algeria, the Democratic Republic of Congo, Egypt, Ethiopia, Kenya, Libya, Niger, Rwanda, Sudan, Tanzania, Uganda, Zimbabwe, and many other countries.

Welcome to Zambia: The Butterfly in the Heart of Africa

http://www.zambiatourism.com/travel/places/victoria.htm

This site, presented by the Zambia National Tourist Board, explores the animals and nature reserves of Zambia, one of the two countries that share Victoria Falls. Click on the links to see waterfalls, crocodiles, elephants, and more.

INDEX

ABOUT THE AUTHORS

Michael Woods is a science and medical journalist in Washington, D.C. He has won many national writing awards. Mary B. Woods is a school librarian. Their past books include the eight-volume Ancient Technology series, the fifteen-volume Disasters Up Close series, and the seven-volume Ancient Wonders of the World books. The Woodses have four children. When not writing, reading, or enjoying their grandchildren, the Woodses travel to gather material for future books.

PHOTO ACKNOWLEDGMENTS

The images in this book are used with the permission of: © age fotostock/SuperStock, pp. 5, 24, 30, 38, 63; © Gerry Ellis/Digital Vision/Getty Images, pp. 6, 9 (top); © Laura Westlund/Independent Picture Service, pp. 7, 15, 25, 33, 43, 53, 61; AP Photo, p. 8; © Ingo Arndt/Minden Pictures/Getty Images, p. 9 (bottom); © Cyril Ruoso/JH Editorial/Minden Pictures/Getty Images, p. 10; The Dian Fossey Gorilla Fund International, www.gorillafund.org, p. 11; © Bruce Davidson/naturepl.com, p. 12; © Konrad Wothe/Minden Pictures/Getty Images, p. 13; © Robert Caputo/Aurora/Getty Images, pp. 14, 18; © Beverly Joubert/National Geographic/Getty Images, p. 16; © Erich Lessing/Art Resource, NY, p. 17 (top); © Werner Forman/Art Resource, NY, p. 17 (bottom); © Trans-World Photos/SuperStock, p. 20; © Eliot Elisofon/Time & Life Pictures/Getty Images, p. 21 (right); © The Bridgeman Art Library/Getty Images, p. 21 (left); © Lloyd Cluff/CORBIS, p. 22; © Alistair Duncan/Dorling Kindersley/Getty Images, p. 23; © Rischgitz/Hulton Archive/Getty Images, p. 26; © Andrew Holt/Photographer's Choice/Getty Images, p. 27; © London Stereoscopic Company/Hulton Archive/Getty Images, p. 28; © Travel Ink/Gallo Images/Getty Images, p. 29 (top), 50; © Chris Simpson/Riser/Getty Images, p. 29 (bottom); © Frans Lemmens/Stone/Getty Images, pp. 32, 72 (bottom center); © DEA/C.SAPPA/De Agostini Picture Library/Getty Images, p. 34; © Sergio Pitaminz/Robert Harding World Imagery/Getty Images, p. 35; © Bernd Mellemann/Alamy, p. 36; © Sylvester Adams/Digital Vision/Getty Images, p. 37; © Frans Lemmens/The Image Bank/Getty Images, p. 39; © Prisma/SuperStock, p. 40 (top); Photograph of the Tree of Ténéré © KrohnPhotos, www.krohn-photos.com, p. 40 (bottom); © Daryl Balfour/Stone/Getty Images, p. 42; © Pete Turner/Stone/Getty Images, p. 44; © CORBIS, p. 45; © Lutz Bongarts/Bongarts/Getty Images, p. 46; © Sisse Brimberg & Cotton Coulson/Getty Images, pp. 47, 51 (bottom); © Marco Longari/AFP/Getty Images, p. 48 (bottom); © Ulrich Doering/Alamy, p. 48 (top); © Stefania Lamberti/Gallo Images/Getty Images, p. 49; © Jake Wyman/Photonica/Getty Images, p. 51 (top); © Michele Falzone/Photographer's Choice/Getty Images, p. 52; © Simon Hadley/Alamy, p. 54 (left); © Angelo Cavalli/Digital Vision/Getty Images, p. 54 (right); © Sylvester Adams/Digital Vision/Getty Images, p. 55; © Visual Arts Library (London)/Alamy, p. 56; © Michele Falzone/Alamy, p. 57; © Martin Harvey/Alamy, p. 58 (left); © Dr. Justin Gerlach, p. 58 (top right); © Ralph Lee Hopkins/National Geographic/Getty Images, p. 58 (bottom right); © Anup Shah/The Image Bank/Getty Images, p. 60; © Winfried Wisniewski/Foto Natura/Minden Pictures/Getty Images, p. 62; © John R. Kreul/Independent Picture Service, p. 64 (top); © TG Stock/Tim Graham Photo Library/Getty Images, p. 64 (bottom); © Suzi Eszterhas/Minden Pictures/Getty Images, p. 65; © Melville B. Grosvenor/National Geographic/Getty Images, p. 66 (top); © Per-Anders Pettersson/Getty Images, p. 66 (bottom); © A. Bayley-Worthington/Hulton Archive/Getty Images, p. 67; © iStockphoto.com/Brian Raisbeck, p. 68 (top); © Mitsuaki Iwago/Minden Pictures/Getty Images, p. 68 (bottom); © Daryl Balfour/Gallo Images/Getty Images, p. 72 (top left); © Sylvain Grandadam/Photographer's Choice/Getty Images, p. 72 (top center); © Ian Murphy/Stone/Getty Images, p. 72 (top right); © Robert Harding/Robert Harding World Imagery/Getty Images, p. 72 (center right); © Skip Brown/National Geographic/Getty Images, p. 72 (bottom left); © Gerry Ellis/Minden Pictures/Getty Images, p. 72 (bottom right).

Front Cover: © Daryl Balfour/Gallo Images/Getty Images (top left); © Robert Harding/Robert Harding World Imagery/Getty Images (top center); © Gerry Ellis/Minden Pictures/Getty Images (top right); © Sylvain Grandadam/Photographer's Choice/Getty Images (center); © Ian Murphy/Stone/Getty Images (bottom left); © Frans Lemmens/Stone/Getty Images (bottom center); © Skip Brown/National Geographic/Getty Images (bottom right).